D0907077

GRIDIRON GREATS
PRO FOOTBALL'S BEST PLAYERS

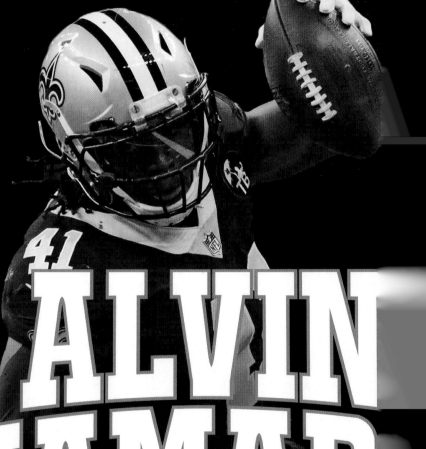

ALVIN KAMARA

BY DONALD PARKER

GRIDIRON GREATS
PRO FOOTBALL'S BEST PLAYERS

AARON DONALD

AARON RODGERS

ALVIN KAMARA

ANTONIO BROWN

DREW BREES

J.J. WATT

JULIO JONES

KHALIL MACK

ODELL BECKHAM JR.

ROB GRONKOWSKI

RUSSELL WILSON

TODD GURLEY

TOM BRADY

VON MILLER

GRIDIRON GREATS
PRO FOOTBALL'S BEST PLAYERS

ALVIN KAMARA

BY DONALD PARKER

MASON CREST

Mason Crest
450 Parkway Drive, Suite D
Broomall, Pennsylvania 19008
(866) MCP-BOOK (toll-free)
www.masoncrest.com

Copyright © 2020 by Mason Crest, an imprint of National Highlights, Inc. All rights reserved. No part of this publication may be reproduced or transmitted in any form or by any means, electronic or mechanical, including photocopying, recording, taping, or any information storage and retrieval system, without permission from the publisher.

First printing
9 8 7 6 5 4 3 2 1

ISBN (hardback) 978-1-4222-4341-1
ISBN (ebook) 978-1-4222-7470-5

Cataloging-in-Publication Data on file with the Library of Congress

NATIONAL
HIGHLIGHTS

Developed and Produced by National Highlights Inc.
Editor: Andrew Luke
Interior and cover design: Jana Rade, impact studios
Production: Michelle Luke

QR CODES AND LINKS TO THIRD-PARTY CONTENT
You may gain access to certain third-party content ("Third-Party Sites") by scanning and using the QR Codes that appear in this publication (the "QR Codes"). We do not operate or control in any respect any information, products, or services on such Third-Party Sites linked to by us via the QR Codes included in this publication, and we assume no responsibility for any materials you may access using the QR Codes. Your use of the QR Codes may be subject to terms, limitations, or restrictions set forth in the applicable terms of use or otherwise established by the owners of the Third-Party Sites. Our linking to such Third-Party Sites via the QR Codes does not imply an endorsement or sponsorship of such Third-Party Sites or the information, products, or services offered on or through the Third-Party Sites, nor does it imply an endorsement or sponsorship of this publication by the owners of such Third-Party Sites.

CONTENTS

CHAPTER 1: GREATEST MOMENTS 7

CHAPTER 2: THE ROAD TO THE TOP 21

CHAPTER 3: ON THE FIELD 35

CHAPTER 4: WORDS COUNT 49

CHAPTER 5: OFF THE FIELD 61

SERIES GLOSSARY OF KEY TERMS 72

FURTHER READING.................... 74

INTERNET RESOURCES............... 75

INDEX............................. 76

PHOTO CREDITS 79

EDUCATIONAL VIDEO LINKS &

AUTHOR BIO...................... 80

KEY ICONS TO LOOK FOR:

Words to Understand: These words with their easy-to-understand definitions will increase the reader's understanding of the text while building vocabulary skills.

Sidebars: This boxed material within the main text allows readers to build knowledge, gain insights, explore possibilities, and broaden their perspectives by weaving together additional information to provide realistic and holistic perspectives.

Educational Videos: Readers can view videos by scanning our QR codes, providing them with additional educational content to supplement the text. Examples include news coverage, moments in history, speeches, iconic sports moments and much more!

Text-Dependent Questions: These questions send the reader back to the text for more careful attention to the evidence presented there.

Research Projects: Readers are pointed toward areas of further inquiry connected to each chapter. Suggestions are provided for projects that encourage deeper research and analysis.

Series Glossary of Key Terms: This back-of-the-book glossary contains terminology used throughout this series. Words found here increase the reader's ability to read and comprehend higher-level books and articles in this field.

WORDS TO UNDERSTAND

INDISPENSABLE – absolutely necessary, crucial, vital, or essential

TANDEM – in association or partnership

TRAJECTORY – a path, progression, or line of development

CHAPTER 1

GREATEST MOMENTS

ALVIN KAMARA'S NFL CAREER

Alvin Kamara was named the top high school football player in the state of Georgia in his senior year of high school. Adept at both rushing and catching the football, he was an all-purpose running back, resulting in many top colleges heavily recruiting him.

After sitting out his freshman year at the University of Alabama due to injury, Kamara encountered some problems that caused him to leave after one year. He transferred and played one year at Hutchinson Community College in Kansas before finishing his college career with two seasons at the University of Tennessee. Kamara was then selected by the New Orleans Saints in the third round of the 2017 NFL (National Football League) draft, behind four other running backs. However, in just two years in the league, Kamara performed as well as or better than those four running backs did, avoiding injuries and playing in four postseason games and two Pro Bowls.

In his first two seasons, Kamara shared the Saints' backfield with veteran Mark Ingram. The two set the NFL record for most all-purpose yards gained by a backfield duo in Kamara's rookie season.

Kamara has made the most of the opportunities that New Orleans has given him, making himself **indispensable** as a player. Sharing a backfield with running back Mark Ingram, the pair rushed and caught passes for a total of 3,094 yards (2,829 m) in 2017, setting the NFL record for the most all-purpose yards by a running back **tandem**. Kamara's efforts that season led the 11–5 Saints to an NFC divisional playoff game against the 13–3 Minnesota Vikings and within five points of his first conference finals game.

The 2018 season saw much of the same from the second-year player. Kamara's 1,592 all-purpose yards helped continue his **trajectory** as one of the top dual threats in the NFL. He rushed and received his way to a second straight Pro Bowl appearance and a chance to lead the Saints to within a questionable pass-inference-no-call away from beating the Los Angeles Rams in the NFC (National Football Conference) final. A win would have given him an opportunity to join a small list of players who have made it to the Super Bowl in their first two NFL seasons.

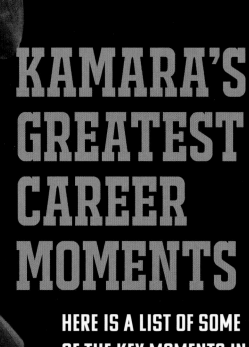

KAMARA'S GREATEST CAREER MOMENTS

HERE IS A LIST OF SOME OF THE KEY MOMENTS IN THE STANDOUT CAREER OF ALVIN KAMARA DURING HIS TIME IN THE NFL SO FAR:

FIRST NFL RUSHING TOUCHDOWN

Kamara's first NFL rushing touchdown was also his first career touchdown. During the September 24, 2017, New Orleans Saints versus Carolina Panthers game, Kamara scored a rushing touchdown, the first of his career, in week three of the season. Kamara finished his rookie campaign with eight rushing touchdowns (TDs)—fourteen total, including one kickoff return TD—just behind the Kansas City Chief's Kareem Hunt and the Jacksonville Jaguars' Leonard Fournette for most rookie rushing yards in 2017.

With 4:42 left in the game, Kamara's twenty-five-yard rush resulted in a touchdown and secured the visiting Saints' victory over the Panthers, 34–13.

FIRST NFL RECEIVING TOUCHDOWN

Just one week after Kamara scored his first NFL rushing touchdown, the all-purpose back scored his first receiving touchdown against the Miami Dolphins on October 1, 2017. The game, a 20–0 victory for the Saints, was held at Wembley Stadium in London, England. The receiving TD was the first of five for Kamara in the 2017 season, when he caught eighty-one passes for 826 yards (755.29 m) as a part of his 700 rushing/800 receiving yards rookie performance.

Kamara caught a twelve-yard pass from quarterback Drew Brees with only 3:57 left to go in the game, sealing the shutout and adding a receiving touchdown to the running back's stat sheet.

FIRST MULTIPLE-TOUCHDOWNS SCORED IN A GAME

As his rookie season wore on, Kamara began to get more touches. He broke through in week nine with two touchdowns against the Tampa Bay Buccaneers on November 5, 2017. He bookended halftime by first catching a thirty-three-yard touchdown pass from Drew Brees with fifty-five seconds to go in the second quarter, then scored the first touchdown for the Saints in the third quarter with a six-yard rush. Kamara would finish the season with three multiple-touchdown games.

Kamara broke several tackles and outran two linebackers, two safeties, and a cornerback after catching a pass from Brees and scampering into the end zone, then celebrated with fans in the crowd. He would have three more two-touchdown games in the 2017 season.

GAME-SAVING PERFORMANCE

Drew Brees threw an eighteen-yard pass to Kamara, who caught it and scored a touchdown with one minute to go in the Saints' week eleven game against Washington. But it wasn't quite enough. Only when Kamara also scored the two-point conversion did he tie the game and send it into overtime on November 19, 2017. It is interesting to note that the two-point conversion that he made was the first of four in his NFL career, which ranks him thirteenth on the all-time career list, three behind leader and Hall of Fame running back Marshall Faulk.

With 7:25 to go in overtime, the Saints' Wil Lutz kicked a twenty-eight-yard field goal to win the game for New Orleans, a victory that would not have been possible without Kamara's touchdown catch and two-point conversion at the end of regulation.

FIRST TOUCHDOWN SCORED IN THE POSTSEASON

The New Orleans Saints went 11–5 in 2017 and played the Carolina Panthers in the NFC wild card game on January 7, 2018. With five minutes to go in the game, Kamara's two-yard rushing touchdown increased the Saints' lead to 31–19 (at 8:24 in the video). Though the Panthers would score again, New Orleans won the game and progressed to the second round of the playoffs.

One of Kamara's opponents in the game was Christian McCaffrey, another running back who was selected ahead of Kamara in the 2017 draft. McCaffrey also scored one touchdown in the game, but it was not enough to give Carolina the victory.

NAMED 2017 AP (ASSOCIATED PRESS) OFFENSIVE ROOKIE OF THE YEAR

Kamara was taken with the sixty-seventh pick (third round) of the 2017 NFL draft. Four running backs were selected ahead of him, including other offensive stars such as running backs (RBs) Leonard Fournette and Christian McCaffrey, and quarterbacks (QBs) Patrick Mahomes and Deshaun Watson, all selected in the first round with the fourth, eighth, tenth, and twelfth picks respectively. On February 3, 2018, at the Orpheum Theatre in Minneapolis, MN, Kamara was honored for his efforts in the 2017 season by being named the AP Offensive Rookie of the Year, besting all of those who were selected before him.

Seahawks Super Bowl champion quarterback Russell Wilson, also a third-round pick (in 2012) from the University of Wisconsin, and his wife, singer Ciara, announced Kamara's Offensive Rookie of the Year award.

THREE TOUCHDOWNS SCORED IN A GAME

On the opening drive of the opening game of the season, Kamara proved that being named the previous year's Offensive Rookie of the Year was no fluke. Against division rival Tampa Bay, on September 9, 2018, Kamara scored a five-yard rushing touchdown for a 7–0 Saints lead. He didn't score again until the last two New Orleans drives, scoring not only a one-yard rushing touchdown with 8:54 to go in the game, but also scoring the two-point conversion with another run. Then just five minutes later, Kamara caught a seven-yard pass from quarterback Drew Brees to score the Saints' fifth touchdown of the day.

Unfortunately, Kamara's three-touchdown day wasn't enough as New Orleans lost to the Buccaneers 48–40. However, the Saints would go on to win their next ten games in a row.

106-YARD KICK RETURN TOUCHDOWN

Even though the Saints lost the game, Kamara all but locked down the Rookie of the Year award with his performance in the week seventeen game on December 31, 2017. With 9:42 to go in the first quarter, Kamara caught a kickoff in the end zone and considered taking a knee for the touchback. Instead, he sprinted 106 yards for a game-tying touchdown, while also setting the record for longest kick return for a touchdown in Saints history.

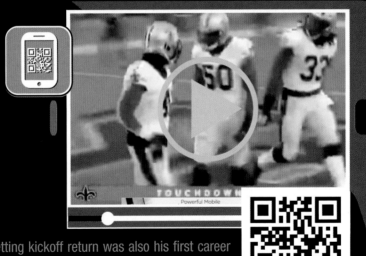

Kamara's record-setting kickoff return was also his first career kick return for a touchdown, as well as the longest kick return of the season in the NFL. He scored a second touchdown later in the same quarter, a seven-yard rush with 2:36 to go.

ARCHIE MANNING 8

PETE MARAVICH 7

JIM FINKS

RICKEY JACKSON 57

DAVE DIXON

EDDIE ROBINSON

Kamara may well be good enough to have his number hanging in the Superdome someday.

The future is certainly bright for this all-around talented running back. Kamara's style and skill at the position can be compared with that of career all-purpose-yards leader Jerry Rice, Brian Mitchell, Walter Payton, LaDainian Tomlinson, and former New Orleans Saints running back Darren Sproles (now of the Philadelphia Eagles). This is pretty good company, considering that Rice, Payton, and Tomlinson are all members of Pro Football's Hall of Fame. At the young age of twenty-three, it is possible, barring a serious injury or significant decline in his skills, that Kamara's name will be among the great Saints players honored in the New Orleans Mercedes-Benz Superdome's Ring of Honor. It is also possible that his name will appear among the greats at the Hall of Fame in Canton, Ohio.

RESEARCH PROJECT:

Kamara returned a kickoff more than 100 yards (91.44 m) for a touchdown in a December 31, 2017, game against the Tampa Bay Buccaneers. The touchdown was part of a remarkable season for Kamara and the run was one for the history books. It was not, however, the longest kickoff in NFL history. Looking through the history of the NFL, find which player holds the record for the longest return yards in the following categories (note: each of these records resulted in a touchdown):

- Kickoff return
- Punt return
- Fumble return
- Field goal attempt return

Name the player, the team played for, the opponent against whom the record was set, the date of the game each of the records was set, and the number of yards for each return.

TEXT-DEPENDENT QUESTIONS:

1. What team did Kamara score his first postseason touchdown against?
2. What is the name of the player whom Kamara shared the backfield with as a member of the New Orleans Saints?
3. What award did Kamara receive at the end of the 2017 NFL season?

WORDS TO UNDERSTAND

ALL-PURPOSE BACK – a running back who is proven to be effective on all downs and all situations

COMBINE – an event at which scouts from the teams in a professional sports league gather to evaluate players in preparation for choosing which players to draft

REDSHIRT – designation given to a college athlete who is unable to participate for that season due to injury or transfer. After the redshirt season is over, the athlete still has four years of college eligibility remaining.

CHAPTER 2

THE ROAD TO THE TOP

ATHLETIC ACCOMPLISHMENTS IN HIGH SCHOOL AND COLLEGE

HIGH SCHOOL

Alvin Kamara was born in the Atlanta suburb of Norcross, GA. In 2012, as a senior, the running back led the Norcross High School Blue Devils to its first Georgia state football championship. That season Kamara rushed for 2,264 yards and twenty-six touchdowns, also catching twenty-two receptions for 286 yards and five touchdowns. The *Atlanta Journal Constitution* named Kamara the high school football player of the year in Georgia, and he was selected to the 2013 Under Armour All-America Game. Only the top 100 high school football players in the United States are selected to compete in the game, typically played each year in early January in Florida.

COLLEGE

Heavily recruited by many top colleges, including Clemson, Auburn, Florida, and Georgia, Kamara was ranked as the number one, **all-purpose back** in the country by 247Sports and number two by Rivals. com. He eventually committed to attend the University of Alabama to play for Coach Nick Saban, who had sent him 105 recruitment letters that arrived on the same day. But Kamara was **redshirted** after a preseason knee injury required surgery, and he was sent to the scout team. By the end of the season, he decided to transfer out of the program.

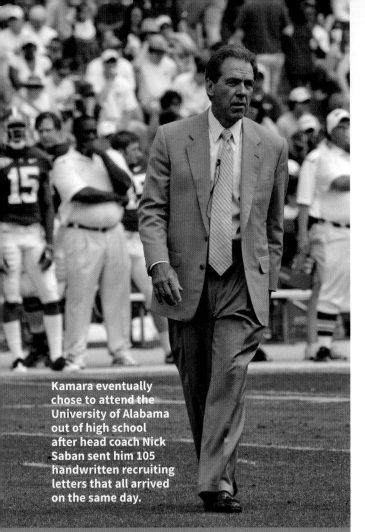

Kamara eventually chose to attend the University of Alabama out of high school after head coach Nick Saban sent him 105 handwritten recruiting letters that all arrived on the same day.

His next stop was Hutchinson Community College in Hutchinson, Kansas. With his knee fully healed, Kamara finished the season with 1,211 rushing yards and twenty-one touchdowns. He was named the Kansas Jayhawk Community College Conference (KJCCC) Offensive Player of the Year in 2014, as well as a National Junior College Athletic Association (NJCAA) All-American. That performance was good enough to once again draw the attention of many elite college programs, and he announced he would return to the SEC, this time to attend the University of Tennessee.

In his two years at the University of Tennessee, Kamara rushed for 1,294 yards and sixteen touchdowns, along with catching seventy-four receptions for 683 yards and seven touchdowns. He also helped lead the Volunteers to victories against Northwestern in the Outback Bowl at the end of the 2015 season, and over Nebraska in the 2016 Music City Bowl. After his junior season, Kamara declared he would enter the 2017 NFL Draft.

By the end of his college career, Kamara had recovered from a variety of setbacks (including knee surgery, being sent down to the Alabama scout team, being suspended from the team before Alabama's appearance in the Sugar Bowl, and being arrested for driving with a suspended license) to earn an invitation to the NFL **Combine** and become a potential high-draft pick. Kamara's stats for his three years in college football are as follows:

Year	Class	Rushes	Rushing Yards	Rushing TDs	Avg Yards per Rush	Receptions	Receiving Yards	Receiving TDs
2014*	FR	172	1,253	18	7.3	18	224	3
2015	SO	107	698	7	6.5	34	291	3
2016	JR	103	596	9	5.8	40	392	4
Totals		382	2,547	34	6.7	92	907	10

His 2014 season was at Hutchinson Community College; 2015 and 2016 seasons were at the University of Tennessee.

Before the draft, many players participate in the NFL's National Pro Scout Combine in Indianapolis, IN, and Kamara was no exception. His results from the Combine included the following:

- Measurements: 5 feet, 10 inches (1.77 m), aproximately 215 (97 kg)
- 40-yard dash: 4.56 seconds
- Vertical jump: 39.5" (1 m)
- Broad jump: 131" (3.32 m)

ALVIN KAMARA
DRAFT DAY

Alvin Kamara was selected by New Orleans with the sixty-seventh pick in the third round of the 2017 NFL Draft.

NFL DRAFT DAY 2017
SIGNIFICANT ACTIONS

- The 2017 NFL Draft was held on the steps of the Philadelphia Museum of Art (made famous in the movie *Rocky*) in Philadelphia, PA, on April 27–29, 2017. This was the first time the draft had been held in Philadelphia since 1961.

- Myles Garrett, a defensive end from Texas A&M University, was the number one overall draft selection, picked by the Cleveland Browns.

- Alvin Kamara was the fifth running back selected in the 2017 NFL Draft.

- The 2017 draft saw a record thirty-seven trades completed, including eleven in the first round.

- A total of 253 players were selected in the draft over three days and seven selection rounds.

- Chad Kelly, a quarterback from the University of Mississippi (Ole Miss), was the last player drafted ("Mr. Irrelevant") in the seventh round by the Denver Broncos.

- The top three positions selected were cornerbacks (thirty-four), wide receivers (thirty-two), and linebackers (twenty-nine). The bottom three positions drafted were placekickers (three), fullbacks (three), and long snappers (one).

- Cincinnati, Minnesota, and Seattle all had the most selections (eleven) in the 2017 draft.

- The New England Patriots had the fewest selections (four) in the 2017 draft.

- The Indianapolis Colts had the fewest selections in the draft, with five.

Kamara was a dominant force in college at the University of Tennessee, as these highlights demonstrate.

@JustBombsProductions

The 2017 NFL Combine took place at Lucas Oil Stadium in Indianapolis.

LUCAS OIL STADIUM

WELCOME TO FD+C

Kamara scored a twenty-four on the Wonderlic Test, which assesses a player's ability to think, learn, follow instructions, and solve problems. His score was the highest of the twenty-four running backs who participated in the Combine.

Kamara was graded an overall A- at the Combine, and the scouts analyzed some of his strengths and weaknesses as follows:

Strengths: "Kamara is a spirited runner with NFL size and speed. Strong lower body provides superior balance. Well-liked inside program and a team leader. Can play on all three downs. Sure-handed pass catcher. Has talent as punt returner."

Weaknesses: "Vision can be hit or miss. Not an instinctive runner. Can be his own worst enemy on third level. With knee injuries in his background, combine medicals could come into play. Needs to tuck ball high and tight to prevent fumbles."

KAMARA VERSUS 2017 NFL RUNNING BACK DRAFT CLASS

Alvin Kamara was the fifth running back selected in the 2017 draft. The four running backs drafted before him were Leonard Fournette (fourth selection, Jacksonville Jaguars), Christian McCaffrey (eighth selection, Carolina Panthers), Dalvin Cook (forty-first selection, Minnesota Vikings), and Joe Mixon (forty-eighth selection, Cincinnati Bengals).

A total of twenty-six running backs were drafted during the 2017 draft. Here is some additional information about the four running backs who were selected ahead of Kamara:

1. Leonard Fournette, Louisiana State University (drafted by the Jacksonville Jaguars, first round, fourth overall selection)—Fournette's NFL career has been up and down due to injuries and behavioral issues. In his rookie season, he ran for 1,040 yards and nine touchdowns, despite missing one game with an

ankle injury and one for violating team rules. He missed seven games in the 2018 season with a hamstring injury and was suspended for one game after brawling with a member of the Buffalo Bills and being ejected from the game. He does, however, hold the NFL record for being the youngest player with a rushing touchdown of at least ninety yards.

2. Christian McCaffrey, Stanford University (drafted by the Carolina Panthers, first round, eighth overall selection)—McCaffrey played in all thirty-two regular season games in his first two years with the Panthers and started all sixteen games in his second season, ending with 1,098 rushing yards and seven touchdowns. Add to that his 107 receptions for 867 yards and another six touchdowns, and McCaffrey broke the Panthers' record for all-purpose yards in one season, with 1,965 yards.

3. Dalvin Cook, Florida State University (drafted by the Minnesota Vikings, second round, forty-first overall selection)—Cook's NFL career got off to a promising start when, in his first professional game, he set the Vikings' rookie debut rushing record with twenty-two carries for 127 yards. But in game four he tore his ACL (anterior cruciate ligament) and was out for the year, returning for the 2018 season with a surgically repaired knee. In eleven games he ran for 615 yards and two touchdowns, and added two more receiving TDs.

4. Joe Mixon, University of Oklahoma (drafted by the Cincinnati Bengals, second round, forty-eighth overall selection)—Mixon overcame the notoriety of an assault charge in college to run for 626 yards and four touchdowns in his rookie season with the Bengals. He doubled those stats in 2018 with 1,168 yards and eight touchdowns, making him the AFC leader in rushing yards for the season.

Top-drafted running back Leonard Fournette (#27), had a great rookie season, but issues on and off the field have led to injuries and suspensions since.

Here are the numbers for the first five running backs taken in the 2017 draft through two full seasons:

Player	Round, Selection	Team	Rushes	Rushing Yards	Rushing TDs	Avg Yards per Rush
Leonard Fournette	1, 4	Jacksonville	401	1,479	14	3.7
Christian McCaffrey	1, 8	Carolina	336	1,533	9	4.6
Dalvin Cook	2, 41	Minnesota	207	969	4	4.7
Joe Mixon	2, 48	Cincinnati	415	1,794	12	4.3
Alvin Kamara	3, 67	New Orleans	314	1,611	22	3.4

Christian McCaffrey is one of four running backs selected ahead of Kamara in the 2017 NFL draft. He went eighth overall to Carolina.

Though he wasn't drafted until the third round, Kamara has performed as well as, or better than, the rest of the 2017 running back class in both total rushing yards and rushing touchdowns. A true all-purpose back, he was the first player in NFL history to both rush for 1,000 yards and tally 1,000 receiving yards in his first twenty professional games. As a result, Kamara was named the NFL Offensive Rookie of the Year after the 2017 season.

Kamara has also performed well in the postseason. In the 2018 Divisional Round, he had seventy-one rushing yards and thirty-five receiving yards in the Saints' victory over the Eagles; the next week he added eleven receptions for ninety-six yards in New Orleans' loss to the Los Angeles Rams. In just two years, Kamara has proven himself to be one of the best, most consistent, and most dependable all-purpose backs in the NFL.

A WALK TO REMEMBER

As a member of the New Orleans Saints, Alvin Kamara plays his home games in the Mercedes-Benz Superdome in downtown New Orleans. He also lives downtown and actually walks through the French Quarter to the Superdome before games, then walks back home to his apartment afterward. He loves the city's vibe, and enjoys soaking up the love from fans, who stop him for hugs and pictures, and banter with him constantly as he makes his way through the streets.

In just two short seasons, Kamara established himself as one of the best all-purpose backs in the NFL.

RESEARCH PROJECT:

After leaving the University of Alabama, Alvin Kamara transferred to Hutchinson Community College for one year before attending the University of Tennessee. Junior colleges are often good stepping-stones for players during their college careers. Looking back at its history, find out how many former Hutchinson Community College players have been drafted by NFL teams. Learn which other teams are members of the Kansas Jayhawk Community College Conference and discover what one of those football teams has recently become well-known for.

TEXT-DEPENDENT QUESTIONS:

1. Where did Rivals.com rank Kamara coming out of high school?
2. How many running backs were selected in the 2017 NFL draft before Alvin Kamara? How many total running backs were drafted?
3. What was Alvin Kamara's score on the Wonderlic Test? How did he score in relation to the other running backs at the Combine?

WORDS TO UNDERSTAND

BYE – the position of a participant in a tournament who advances to the next round without playing

CULMINATE – to reach the highest, or a climactic or decisive point

MISMATCHES – an unsuitable contest between two or more parties

CHAPTER 3

ON THE FIELD

KAMARA'S NFL ACCOMPLISHMENTS

From high school and college and on into the NFL, Kamara has achieved many things in his football career. His rookie season in the NFL started slowly, as he did not score his first professional touchdown until week three. Since he got started, however, he has been almost unstoppable. Kamara eventually led all rookies with eighty-one receptions (the third most by a rookie running back in NFL history), as well as in total touchdowns (fourteen). In his second year, he set a New Orleans Saints record with a 106-yard kickoff return touchdown, and by the end of the season, he had joined Hall of Fame legend Jim Brown as the only player aged twenty-three or younger to score three or more touchdowns in three different games in one season.

Additionally, Kamara, as a rookie in 2017, became a member of an exclusive club when he gained 700 receiving yards and 800 rushing yards in a single season. He is the first Saint, third rookie, and eleventh player in NFL history to accomplish this.

Kamara played four playoff games in his first two seasons but came up short of playing in the Super Bowl in either season.

Kamara also averaged more than six yards (5.49 m) per rush as a rookie. This average is the highest for any NFL rookie in the history of the game (as well as a record for any Saints player) and, since 1980, the third highest in the league. Rushing in tandem with Mark Ingram, the pair became the first in which each player recorded more than 1,500 (1,371.6 m) all-purpose yards. Kamara is the only player in NFL history to record 1,000 yards (914.4 m) in both receiving and rushing in his first twenty games as an NFL running back.

Kamara's statistics in two short years put him on par with some of the game's greatest players. He reached 500 yards rushing in 2017 in just eleven games. This mark is the fastest since Herschel Walker accomplished a similar rookie mark in 1986. Kamara earned his first Pro Bowl invite with teammate Mark Ingram, making them the first running back pair in NFL history to be named together. His other NFL accomplishments are nothing short of remarkable:

- Only the second rookie in NFL history to run for five rushing touchdowns, five touchdown receptions, and a kickoff return for a touchdown.
- Led all rookies with eighty-one receptions (third most by a rookie running back in NFL history) and fourteen total touchdowns.
- As a rookie, ranked second among all NFL players with 1,554 yards from scrimmage.
- Scored three TDs in a game three separate times.

KAMARA ON THE GRIDIRON

Kamara is considered an all-purpose back, skilled in rushing, receiving, and even blocking for other offensive players when called upon to do so. After only two NFL seasons, Kamara's performance showed that he has the potential to be one of the best all-purpose running backs in professional football. In fact, his receiving stats in his first two seasons were as good as, or even better than some of the best wide receivers in football history.

Kamara's playing style is a throwback to a time when offensive players did more than what their position requires today. He is more than a traditional running back. Kamara has the ability not only to make defenders miss him when carrying the ball, but also to cause those players covering him to simply watch

In his first two seasons, Kamara recorded three three-touchdown games.

GRIDIRON GREATS

ALVIN KAMARA
NEW ORLEANS SAINTS

RUNNING BACK

ALVIN KAMARA

Date of birth: July 25, 1995 **Height:** 5 feet, 10 inches (1.78 m) **Weight:** Approximately 215 pounds (97 kg) **Drafted** in the third round in 2017 (sixty-seventh pick overall) by the New Orleans Saints **College:** University of Tennessee at Knoxville

CAREER

GAMES	RUSH	RUYDS	RUTD	REC	REYDS	RETD
31	314	1611	22	162	1535	9

- Named to two Pro Bowls (2017–2018)
- Named second- team All-Pro in 2018
- Named AP NFL Offensive Rookie of the Year in 2017
- Named to NFL's All-Rookie Team for 2017 season
- Named to NFL Top 100 for 2018 season—Ranked #20
- Played high school football at Norcross High School (Norcross, GA) (nickname: "Blue Devils"), 2011–2014

RUNNING BACK

Kamara's ability to excel at both running and catching the ball is a throwback to an era of more versatile running backs.

him blow by after making a spectacular grab. If that were not enough, he is also an excellent kick returner, making him a threat to take the return for a score every time.

When looking at Kamara's first two NFL seasons, here is how his receiving numbers compare against the first two seasons of some of the greatest wide receivers the league has seen in its 100 years:

Player	G	Receptions	Rcv Yds	Rcv TD
James Lofton*	32	100	1,786	10
Marvin Harrison*	30	127	1,702	14
Alvin Kamara	**31**	**162**	**1,535**	**9**
Terrell Owens*	32	95	1,456	12
Steve Largent*	28	87	1,348	14

*Member of Pro Football Hall of Fame

Kamara's numbers against the top all-purpose running backs are just as favorable (comparing each player's first two seasons in the NFL):

Player	G	Rush Attempts	Rush Yds	Rush TD
Emmitt Smith*	32	606	2,500	23
Marshall Faulk*	32	603	2,360	22
Frank Gore†	30	439	2,303	11
Walter Payton*	27	507	2,069	20
Alvin Kamara†	31	314	1,611	22

*Member of Pro Football Hall of Fame
†Currently active

Another reason for Kamara's early success in the NFL is that a team that knew how to use his talents drafted him. A true all-purpose back, Kamara has excelled in Saints' coach Sean Payton's "Joker" offense, which employs a multi-purpose back who can play from a variety of field positions to create **mismatches**. This hybrid role requires the player to run complex routes, be speedy and difficult to tackle, line up as a receiver in the slot or in the backfield, and even play on special teams as a kick returner. Kamara fits the bill on all these elements. His proper use in

Kamara had more receiving yards in his first two seasons at running back than Hall of Famer Terrell Owens did in his first two seasons at wide receiver.

Kamara has fit in perfectly with the Saints, who play a system that meshes perfectly with his skill set.

the Joker-style offense **culminated** in his being named rookie of the year in 2017.

Kamara has been able to stand out at every level, starting in high school and then in his time at Hutchinson Community College, and even as a backup at the University of Tennessee. Turning in complete offensive performances (both rushing and receiving) has always been a part of his game. It is no surprise that Kamara has become successful at the professional level. He probably would have excelled playing for another coach or in another system given his work ethic on the field and his talent level. However, playing for the Saints has put Kamara in the best position to exceed expectations.

Here are the regular season rushing and receiving stats for Kamara's first two seasons (2017–2018):

Year	G	GS	RushYds	RushTD	RecYds	RecTD	TotalYds
2017*†‡	16	3	728	8	826	5	1554
2018*	15	13	883	14	709	4	1592
Career	31	16	1,611	22	1,535	9	3,146

*Pro Bowl selection
†Second-team All-Pro
‡All-Rookie team selection

KAMARA IN THE PLAYOFFS

Some professional football players go their entire careers without winning, let alone appearing in, any postseason games. In his first two years in the NFL, however, Kamara appeared in four playoff games.

In the 2017 season, the Saints won the NFC South with an 11–5 record, resulting in their first postseason appearance in four years. On January 7, 2018—Wild Card Sunday—the Saints hosted the Carolina Panthers in the Mercedes-Benz Superdome. In New Orleans' 31–26 victory, Kamara scored the team's last touchdown, a two-yard run with 5:08 minutes to go in the game.

The following Sunday, the Saints traveled to Minneapolis, where they faced the Minnesota Vikings, winners of the NFC North. Kamara contributed a fourteen-yard touchdown reception for the Saints; however, Minnesota scored a touchdown as time expired on a play in which Saints' safety Marcus Williams badly missed an easy tackle. This allowed the Vikings to defeat New Orleans in stunning fashion. The game came to be known as the "Minneapolis Miracle."

Kamara played his first career playoff game on his home field in the Superdome on January 7, 2018.

Former teammates Kamara and Ingram were a running back powerhouse in the NFL. Going by the nickname "Boom and Zoom," here are the highlights of the two seasons they played together in New Orleans.

THE BROTHERHOOD OF KAMARA AND INGRAM

Kamara has thrived in New Orleans for many reasons. One of those is his relationship with fellow running back Mark Ingram. Both attended the University of Alabama; Ingram won the Heisman Trophy and national championship there in 2009, while Kamara transferred away after being redshirted during his freshman year. Instead of competing for playing time with the Saints, Ingram took the rookie Kamara under his wing and served as his mentor since Kamara arrived. They gave their postgame interviews together in front of their lockers, which are next to each other. At the end of the 2017 season, they became the first running backs from the same team to make the Pro Bowl together since 1975. At the beginning of the 2018 season, when Ingram was suspended for four games for violating the NFL's policy on performance-enhancing drugs, Kamara picked up the slack until his partner returned. Later that year, they became the first running back duo to each record 1,500 total yards in NFL history. When Ingram left for Baltimore in 2019, Kamara shared his feelings in an Instagram post:

"Probably the smoothest first 2 years an NFL player has ever had and I owe a lot of it to you brother," Kamara wrote. "Thank you from the bottom of my heart."

Kamara is the only player in NFL history to record 1,000 yards (914.4 m) in both receiving and rushing in his first twenty games as an NFL running back.

The Saints improved their 2017 record by finishing the 2018 regular season 13–3. They again won the NFC South, but this time earned a **bye** during Wild Card weekend. Their first playoff game was Sunday, January 13, 2019, when they hosted the reigning Super Bowl champions, the Philadelphia Eagles. New Orleans' 20–14 victory ensured they would advance to the NFC championship game the following week.

In the Superdome on January 20, 2019, the Saints fell to the Los Angeles Rams in overtime, 26–23, a controversial finish due to a missed pass interference call late in regulation time. While Kamara played in both games, he did not score any touchdowns, though he made his presence felt with a game-high eleven receptions for ninety-six yards, including one twenty-one-yard catch in the first half. As a running back, he was stifled by the Rams' defense, but as a receiver, three of his receptions resulted in first downs for the Saints.

Here is a look at Kamara's first four playoff game totals:

Year	G	GS	RushYds	RushTD	RecYds	RecTD	TotalYds
2017	2	1	66	1	5	72	1
2018	2	1	86	0	15	131	0
Career	4	2	152	1	20	203	1

RESEARCH PROJECT:

Kamara's on-field performance in 2017 won him the Offensive Rookie of the Year award in the NFL. Find out what other players have won either the Offensive or Defensive Rookie of the Year awards in the past fifteen years, and how each of those winners was determined. Learn what corporation sponsors a separate Rookie of the Year award, when they started presenting the award, and how that winner is selected. Compare the two to see if the winners are the same. Then trace the winners' paths through the NFL—whether they have gone on to win other awards, play on a Super Bowl team, or are even still in the NFL. Create a chart to present your findings.

TEXT-DEPENDENT QUESTIONS:

1. What fellow running back on the Saints became a mentor to Alvin Kamara?
2. What is the "Joker" position, and why is it important to the Saints?
3. What NFL Hall of Fame running back did Kamara join in the record books in the 2018 season?

WORDS TO UNDERSTAND

INNOVATIVE – characterized by, tending to, or introducing a new idea, method

PERSONA – the personality that a person (such a celebrity or politician) projects in public

PLATITUDE – a banal, trite, or stale remark

VIRAL – quickly and widely spread or popularized especially by means of social media

CHAPTER 4

WORDS COUNT

In today's world, athletes are more connected to their fans than ever before. Whether speaking formally in a press conference or informally via social media, some athletes can be counted on to provide sound bites that quickly go **viral** ("Quote Machine"), while others rely on tried-and-true responses ("Cliché City"). Here are ten quotes, compiled in part from various websites, including Twitter and Instagram, with some insight as to the context of what Kamara is talking about or referencing:

> **I think it's a lot of credit to the system. As an organization, as a coach, you get players and you find the best ways to use their skills. Sometimes you don't do it right, sometimes you do. I'm just grateful I'm in a position where my skills are being used.**

Kamara thinks Saints head coach Sean Payton has done a great job establishing an offensive system that makes use of Kamara's skills.

As a rookie, Kamara was racking up both rushing and receiving yards, as a result of playing the multipurpose "Joker" position in the Saints' offense. No matter what it was called, it worked, and Kamara was thankful. His ability to excel in Coach Payton's **innovative** offense has led to him being recognized as one of the best all-purpose running backs in the NFL. He has played in back-to-back Pro Bowls even though he has yet to rush for more than 1,000 yards (941.4 m) in a season. He recognizes that the right team drafted him and that he has the right coach to help him best contribute on the field.
Rating: Quote Machine

A lot of people don't really believe it. But we don't need anybody to believe in us but us.

In Kamara's rookie season, the Saints were 10–4 but still considered underdogs to win in the playoffs. When asked about this on ESPN, Kamara revealed his team's feelings about those doubts. His arrival in New Orleans has contributed to the team making it to the divisional playoffs in 2017, his rookie season, and the NFC conference finals in 2018. He knows that the Saints are an up-and-coming team. Whether the national media wants to believe that the Saints are a good team or not is of no concern to Kamara. He and his teammates believe that they are on the way to winning another championship for the Saints. **Rating: Quote Machine**

I don't just play football. I'm Alvin. Alvin Kamara. I happen to play football.

With this statement to Aaron Dodson of *The Undefeated* made at the end of his rookie year, Kamara wanted to remind fans that he is multifaceted both on and off the field. He may be developing a reputation on the gridiron as a multifaceted, all-purpose running back. He may very well go on and have one of the greatest careers at the position and even make it to the Pro Football Hall of Fame. However, Kamara also wants people—fans and otherwise—to understand that he is also a person, not just the player Alvin Kamara. Football has become an important aspect of his life and has turned into his career. He is careful to point out that this isn't what defines him as a person and that there is a lot more to him than his ability to carry a ball. **Rating: Quote Machine**

> **They're hungry, we all know what the situation is, we have a "next man up" mentality. Everybody is working hard, and guys know they have to make plays, so we are going to do that.**

Kamara's fellow running back, Mark Ingram, was suspended for the first four games of the 2018 season. When asked how the team would respond, he resorted to a typical **platitude** ("next man up"). This cliché is a common phrase used in all sports. What it means is that a professional team contains players who, when called upon, must be ready to step up and contribute, regardless of the circumstances. Although Kamara and Ingram worked together as a **duo** (the first to be named to the same All-Pro game), the suspension required Kamara as a second-year player to adopt the "next man up" mentality and step up his game for the Saints to win—which they did. **Rating: Cliché City**

Kamara had his second three-touchdown game against the New York Giants on September 30, 2018. He was able to toot his own horn and give credit to his offensive line at the same time with this gem. He recognized that if it wasn't for the hard work and effort of his offensive linemen, it would not have been possible for him to achieve one, let alone two three-touchdown games. He is more than generous in his praise of his fellow teammates and knows that because of the way they handled their business, he was able to walk into the end zone, practically untouched. **Rating: Quote Machine**

> **It was a perfect look. The O-line handled their business. I could've scored that ball with my eyes closed.**

DeShaun Watson is one of a handful of 2017 rookies whom Kamara beat out for Offensive Rookie of the Year.

> **There's time for everything, and right now it's football time and I'm locked back in on my team.**

Kamara went into the Saints' training camp in 2018 as the reigning AP Offensive Rookie of the Year, which can be stressful for a young player. When asked how he handles that stress, he replied with a straightforward, yet somewhat standard, answer. Winning awards and being recognized as the top offensive player as a rookie were some things he celebrated as they happened. He is proud of the fact that he won these honors despite being drafted in the third round of the draft with the sixty-seventh pick. He beat out first round picks Leonard Fournette (RB), Deshaun Watson (QB), and Patrick Mahomes (QB) for the top offensive honors. Going into the 2018 season, however, his focus was on how he could help the Saints improve on their 11–5 finish in 2017 and reach Super Bowl LII. His attention was on his team and not the awards he had won the year prior. **Rating: Cliché City**

"Yeah, that's legendary material right there. You know when you were a kid and you see all those guys with bobbleheads and you're like, "Dang I want a bobblehead." That's one thing, when I was younger growing up, playing sports I wanted a bobblehead. So, to see that is cool.

If Kamara's career maintains its course, his bobblehead may one day join ones like these at the National Bobblehead Hall of Fame in Milwaukee.

Many athletic teams produce bobbleheads of the star players, and the Saints are no exception, Kamara clearly liked his. Seeing his image cast as a bobblehead is the fulfillment of a dream for him. Having the bobblehead said to him that he has finally arrived as a player and has done the right things in his career to be recognized in such a fashion by his team. As he continues to develop his skills, there will likely be many more bobbleheads honoring him as a player. **Rating: Quote Machine**

YOU CAN TAKE THE MAN OUT OF THE GAME, BUT YOU CAN'T TAKE THE GAME OUT OF THE MAN

A commercial that aired before Super Bowl LIII on Sunday, February 3, 2019, was a celebration of the NFL's 100th season. Taking place at a formal dinner hosted by NFL commissioner Roger Goodell, the gathering, attended by scores of NFL stars past and present, soon turned into a mad scramble for the golden football.

Kamara and quarterback Drew Brees represented the Saints in a Super Bowl LIII commercial that featured NFL legends past and present.

[Players] put on capes in the league. They got a character. They got a persona they fulfill, a brand. I don't see a problem with it. Maximize your pockets. But what I put on, I ain't gotta put on no cape. I just do what I feel. That's what draws people. This isn't an act.

Kamara is known throughout New Orleans and the league as authentic, and as one who often acts on instinct. This statement to Master Tesfatsion of *Bleacher Report* reflects that authenticity and his tendency to act on his feelings, making it pure Kamara. He doesn't feel it necessary to take on a different **persona** in order to impress people or make them like him more. He feels that his efforts on the gridiron have more than impressed fans in New Orleans and that as long as he stays true to himself and his character, he will be able to draw in more fans for being an original, not a character. **Rating: Quote Machine**

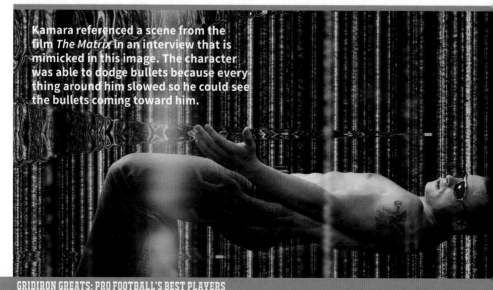

Kamara referenced a scene from the film *The Matrix* in an interview that is mimicked in this image. The character was able to dodge bullets because everything around him slowed so he could see the bullets coming toward him.

I think that was a stepping-stone. I was in the ... pokeball in 'Bama, and I... evolved into some other [Pokémon]...Charizard.

When asked by Tesfatsion about leaving the University of Alabama after one year, Kamara compared himself to a Pokémon character. Who else in the NFL does that? His time at Alabama was not the best for him but it certainly was a learning experience. He grew as a person between the time he left Alabama and entered Tennessee, with a stop at junior college in Kansas. The pokeball reference is how he felt about his time at Alabama and the character Charizard is what he feels he has matured into as a person and as a feared competitor. **Rating: Quote Machine**

Kamara described to reporters how he sees the field while running and picking off defenders one by one—then watching himself later on game video, referencing *The Matrix*, a 1999 film starring Keanu Reeves as the lead character Neo. Neo developed an ability to see everything around him in slow motion, which is how Kamara thinks he sometimes sees the field as plays develop. **Rating: Quote Machine**

I go into *Matrix* mode—him, him, him ... I'm like, "I see what I did there." It was an a-ha moment.

ALVIN KAMARA AND THE MEDIA

Kamara has an extensive social media presence. He has nearly a quarter of a million followers on Twitter, and almost three-quarters of a million followers on Instagram. Both sites are opportunities for him to share photos, thoughts, and information with fans and the public.

In fact, when Kamara first tweeted about his favorite candy, Airheads, in 2017, he notified football fans in New Orleans and nationwide about his love of the sweet treat. Ever since, Kamara has handed out Airheads on the sidelines to teammates whenever he has scored a touchdown. Fans have even begun buying the candy before games as a sort of good luck charm. When the company that makes Airheads, Perfetti Van Melle, heard about the taffy-like candy's newfound popularity in New Orleans, they sent Kamara a large supply to ensure he could continue to share them. When he won Offensive Rookie of the Year, they purchased a billboard in New Orleans with the congratulatory message, "Now, that's how you play delicious!"

Kamara has also been featured in a video series for Airheads entitled, "Play by Play." The candy company took the relationship to the next level, however, when they offered to create a new flavor specifically for Kamara. He jumped at the chance and selected Watermelon Zoom, a "kicked-up" version of his favorite flavor. The candy's black-and-gold wrapper features Kamara's face, as well as his signature, but was not made available for sale to the general public. Rather, all inventory was sent directly to Kamara so that he could hand them out to family, friends, teammates, and anyone else he chose. They have since become as sought-after as Willy Wonka's golden ticket.

An NFL player having his own candy has happened before. Former Seahawks and Raiders running back Marshawn Lynch is featured on the "Marshawn's Pack" of Skittles, the fruity candy he is known to eat during football games.

RESEARCH PROJECT:

Kamara, along with Saints quarterback Drew Brees, appeared in the all-star Super Bowl commercial announcing the celebration of the NFL's 100th season. The commercial was an audience favorite, featuring players from different decades of the game, going as far back as the 1950s. The commercial even performed a take on the famous "Immaculate Reception" featuring Pittsburgh Steelers Hall of Fame RB Franco Harris. Find out what year the NFL was founded, in what city, and by whom. Learn what cities hosted the original NFL teams and whether any of them still exist today.

TEXT-DEPENDENT QUESTIONS:

1. How many touchdowns did Kamara score against the New York Giants on September 30, 2018?

2. How many total followers does Kamara have on the social media channels Twitter and Instagram?

3. What is Kamara's favorite candy?

WORDS TO UNDERSTAND

ECCENTRIC – deviating from conventional or accepted usage or conduct, especially in odd or whimsical ways

INFRACTION – a violation

MIND-SET – a mental attitude or inclination

CHAPTER 5

OFF THE FIELD

KAMARA AT HOME

Alvin Mentian Kamara was born on July 25, 1995, in Norcross, GA, a city of 16,000 residents that is twenty miles (32.19 km) northeast of the city of Atlanta. His mother, Adama, who is from the African country of Liberia, raised him on her own in Norcross. Kamara also has an older sister named Garmai K. Momolu (now a public relations professional in Los Angeles).

After the Saints drafted him in 2017, he chose to make the city of New Orleans his home and found a mentor in teammate Mark Ingram. Ingram, who was the Saints' 2018 nominee for the Walter Payton Man of the Year Award for community service, worked with Kamara off the field to have a great impact on the residents in New Orleans. Ingram passed the torch when he signed as a free agent in Baltimore after the 2018 season. Now Kamara will continue to donate his time and money to a variety of local schools and charities.

The festive, easygoing, fun-loving vibe of New Orleans has meshed well with Kamara's unique personality.

Kamara has come a long way from Norcross, GA, and enjoys being a part of the New Orleans culture. His **eccentric** behavior seems a perfect fit for the "Big Easy," a nickname given to the city for its easygoing lifestyle. Kamara in every way embraces a popular expression heard around town in French, *Laissez les bon temps rouler*, which means in English, "Let the good times roll." He is so easygoing that he once took time to hop aboard a garbage truck and drive around town with local trash collectors, assisting them in their jobs and bringing smiles to the faces of Saints fans.

It is doubtful that any NFL city other than New Orleans would be as much a fit for Kamara's personality. He would probably be a bit more restrained if he had been selected by his hometown team, the Atlanta Falcons, and probably would not be able to find enough "weird" things to get into if he were to play for the Cleveland Browns or Green Bay Packers. New Orleans has proven a perfect match for Kamara and a

ONE OF A KIND

In a city known for eccentricity, Alvin Kamara fits right in. A self-described "weird" kid in school, in college he grew out his hair and began wearing a stud in his left nostril. But when everyone else started piercing their noses, he took it a step further and got his septum pierced. Instead of the regulation mouth guard, he wears a gold grill. Now, fans at Saints games wear fake gold teeth, dreadlocks, and bull nose rings in appreciation.

On his Twitter account he has posted photos of his full-leg tattoos. Instead of living in the suburbs and driving to and from games in a flashy car, he lives downtown and walks through the French Quarter to the Superdome. And he has become as well known for his candy of choice, Airheads (favorite flavor: watermelon), as he is for his on-field performance.

Most players wouldn't wear a ski mask and camouflage while being interviewed about earning the NFC's top playoff seed. Then again, most players aren't Alvin Kamara, where dressing that way is not at all unusual!

place he looks to call home for some time to come. Known for its annual Mardi Gras celebration, its Jazz Festival, and all kinds of exciting things to see and do, especially for a young athlete like Kamara, he finds that he fits in well and feels at home in New Orleans. He has been known to walk from his home near the French Quarter to games at the Saints' downtown stadium. Locals greet him warmly and are appreciative of the effort he puts out each week on the gridiron, as well as his willingness to embrace and be a part of the community.

FRIENDS IN HIGH PLACES

While Kamara's high school dreams included becoming a professional football player, three of his friends—Quavious, Kirshnik, and Kiari—dreamt of becoming famous rappers. That is what they did: they are now known as Quavo, Takeoff, and

Offset, or collectively as Migos. That friendship, though, didn't stop Kamara from making a cameo in the music video for another friend, Drake's "In My Feelings," which was filmed in New Orleans.

KAMARA ON EDUCATION

Kamara initially committed to play for Coach Nick Saban at the University of Alabama in Tuscaloosa, AL. Alabama, as it is referred to, is the flagship of the University of Alabama system and is the oldest of the public universities in the state (founded in 1820). His year on campus was not a successful one as he was injured and redshirted by Coach Saban. After his freshman year, Kamara chose to transfer to junior college, Hutchinson Community College, located in Hutchinson, KS (nickname: "Blue Dragons"). Hutchinson is a two-year, community and area vocational school that offers courses designed for the award of an associate degree.

Kamara played just one season with the Blue Dragons to get back on track with his college career. At the end of the season, he

In 2018, recording artist Drake released the video for his song "In My Feelings," in which Kamara appeared.

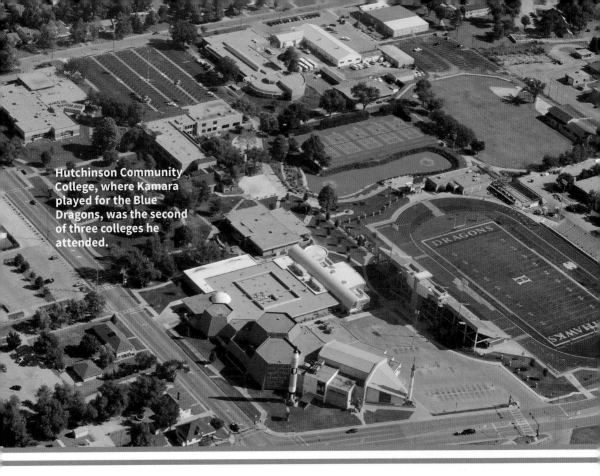

Hutchinson Community College, where Kamara played for the Blue Dragons, was the second of three colleges he attended.

received interest from recruiters at both the University of Georgia at Athens (nickname: "Bulldogs") and the University of Tennessee at Knoxville (nickname: "Volunteers"). With three years of eligibility remaining, he chose to resume his upper-division collegiate football career at Tennessee, where he played for two seasons. He decided to leave with an additional year of eligibility left to enter the 2017 NFL Draft. He didn't graduate from Tennessee prior to being drafted but with more than three years of college work under his belt (plus his year of junior college work), he is close to completing a degree should he decide at any point before or after the end of his NFL career to finish his degree requirements.

IN THE COMMUNITY

HOW THE GRINCH (ALMOST) STOLE CHRISTMAS

When the Saints hosted the Atlanta Falcons in New Orleans on Christmas Eve 2017, Kamara knew he wanted to do something special to celebrate the season. Despite the NFL's strict rules on uniforms, he wore a pair of red cleats made to look like a Christmas stocking, complete with jingle bells and his name written on them in script.

After the game, when it was rumored that Kamara would be penalized for the **infraction**, his then-teammate Mark Ingram pleaded with the NFL, "Don't be a Grinch," but to no avail. Kamara was fined $6,079 for the violation (which went to the NFL Player Care Foundation and the Players Assistance Trust), but he wanted to make a local impact as well. So, he set up a GoFundMe page to ask for additional charitable funds.

As he wrote on the page, "Unfortunately The Grinch stole Christmas!! After the game I said that I would make a gofundme for the fine and donate the proceeds to charity sooooo.... here we are! A donation will be made to Willie Hall playground's recreational department to provide cleats for their youth football programs." The campaign eventually exceeded its goal of $5,000, raising $6,268 for needy children of New Orleans.

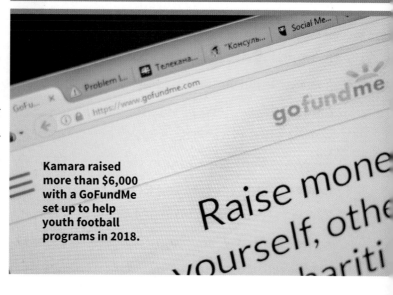

Kamara raised more than $6,000 with a GoFundMe set up to help youth football programs in 2018.

KAMARA MAKES HAPPY CAMPERS
OF YOUTH FOOTBALL PLAYERS

In the summer after Kamara won the NFL's Offensive Rookie of the Year award, he held the first annual Alvin Kamara Rookie of the Year Football Camp for youth ages 7–18 in Chattanooga, TN, on June 23, 2018. Other University of Tennessee alumni such as Josh Malone, Cam Sutton, and Jalen Reeves-Maybin joined him. They ran drills despite a light rain, gave out T-shirts, signed autographs, and then took the nearly thirty kids on a shopping spree.

The next month, Kamara held another free youth football camp, this time at Tad Gormley Stadium in New Orleans for about 150 kids. "It's not an easy camp," Kamara told the *Times-Picayune*. "If you're out here, you're out here to work. I'm not going easy on anybody. If you mess up my cone or my ladder, I need pushups... You got to do it right. That's why we're out here." In addition to motivating the children to excel, Kamara also invited a local high school football team and their coaches to work at the camp.

Kamara surprised a high school coach in New Orleans with Super Bowl tickets in appreciation for his efforts to make sure his players are safe.

KAMARA REWARDS COACH WITH TRIP OF A LIFETIME

In October 2018, the Saints were still in the thick of the playoff hunt and hoped to make a trip to Super Bowl LIII, being held that year in Kamara's hometown of Atlanta. He already knew someone who definitely would be attending the big game.

Kamara surprised Brice Brown, head football coach at Edna Karr High School in New Orleans, with Super Bowl LIII tickets. Coach Brown has made it his mission to ensure his players literally survive high school. In 2016, one of his former players, Tollette "Tonka" George, was shot to death, which caused Coach Brown to change his coaching **mind-set**. He now calls his players every night to make sure they are safe, and Kamara and the Saints have recognized him for his efforts.

KAMARA GIVES THANKS AND GIVES AWAY TURKEYS

One week before Thanksgiving 2018, Kamara teamed up with New Orleans businessman Larry Morrow to host their first annual Turkey Giveaway and Thanksgiving Feast. Local grocery store Winn-Dixie provided 800 turkeys, which Kamara and volunteers gave away in just a half-hour at Stallings Playground in New Orleans' Seventh Ward.

THE MARKETING OF ALVIN KAMARA

Agent Damarius Bilbo of Revolution Sports Group represents Kamara. Bilbo is a former quarterback/wide receiver (QB/WR) who played college football at Georgia Tech University (nickname: "Yellow Jackets"), located in Kamara's hometown of Atlanta. He was an undrafted free agent who spent one season (2006) with the Dallas Cowboys as a defensive back, before leaving the game and becoming a sports agent. Revolution is based in Chicago, IL, and represents such sports and entertainment talent as WRs

Jarvis Landry of the Cleveland Browns and T. J. Jones of the Detroit Lions.

The Super Bowl LII commercial celebrating the NFL's 100th anniversary is probably the biggest commercial Kamara has participated in to date. He has also been doing some local work in support of small businesses in New Orleans, such as his appearance dressed as a trash collector working for the Sidney Torres IV trash-collection company.

SALARY INFORMATION

The New Orleans Saints drafted Kamara with the sixty-seventh pick of the 2017 NFL draft. He signed a rookie contract for four years (2017–2020) for a total value of $3.8 million, which included a $972,772 signing bonus over the four years ($243,193 per year).

YEAR	SALARY	ROSTER BONUS	SIGNING BONUS	TOTAL
2017	$465,000	$0	$243,193	$708,193
2018	$635,000	$0	$243,193	$878,193
2019	$807,500	$0	$243,193	$1,050,693
2020	$977,500	$0	$243,193	$1,220,693
TOTAL	$2,885,000	$0	$972,772	$3,857,772

Kamara has chosen to spend his money conservatively, remembering how things were when he grew up. The most expensive item that he owns may just be the gold grill that he wears in his mouth.

Kamara has had made a big splash in his short time in the NFL. He has quickly established himself as one of the most complete offensive weapons in the league. He is a dual threat, both running and receiving the football. Along with Super Bowl champion QB Drew Brees and two-time Pro Bowl WR Michael Thomas, they have made the New Orleans Saints a feared opponent. Time will tell just how many all-purpose yards Kamara will record as his promising career continues to soar.

RESEARCH PROJECT:

Every year, each NFL team nominates one player for the Walter Payton NFL Man of the Year Award, which is presented during the Super Bowl. The winner of the award is recognized for excellence on the field and outstanding community service off the field. Find out who Walter Payton was and why the award was renamed for him in 1999. Learn who has won the award in the past fifteen years, and what causes those players championed.

TEXT-DEPENDENT QUESTIONS:

1.   What country is Alvin Kamara's mother from?
2.   How much was Alvin Kamara fined for wearing special cleats during a Christmas Eve game?
3.   What musical group's members were friends with Alvin Kamara in high school?

blitz – a defensive strategy in which one or more linebackers or defensive backs, in addition to the defensive line, attempt to overwhelm the quarterback's protection by attacking from unexpected locations or situations.

cornerbacks – the defenders primarily responsible for preventing the offenses wide receivers from catching passes, accomplished by remaining as close to the opponent as possible during pass routes. Cornerbacks are usually the fastest players on the defense.

defensive backs – a label applied to cornerbacks and safeties, or the secondary in general.

end zone – an area 10 yards deep at either end of the field bordered by the goal line and the boundaries.

field goal – an attempt to kick the ball through the uprights, worth three points. It is taken by a specialist called the *place kicker*. Distances are measured from the spot of the kick plus 10 yards for the depth of the end zone.

first down – the first play in a set of four downs, or when the offense succeeds in covering 10 yards in the four downs.

fumble – when a player loses possession of the ball before being tackled, normally by contact with an opponent. Either team may recover the ball. The ground cannot cause a fumble.

goal line – the line that divides the end zones from the rest of the field. A touchdown is awarded if the ball breaks the vertical plane of the goal line while in possession or if a receiver catches the ball in the end zone.

huddle – a gathering of the offense or defense to communicate the upcoming play decided by the coach.

interception – a pass caught by a defensive player instead of an offensive receiver. The ball may be returned in the other direction.

lateral – a pass or toss behind the originating player to a teammate as measured by the lines across the field. Although the offense may only make one forward pass per play, there is no limit to the number of laterals at any time.

line of scrimmage – an imaginary line, determined by the ball's location before each play, that extends across the field from sideline to sideline. Seven offensive players must be on the line of scrimmage, though the defense can set up in any formation. Forward passes cannot be thrown from beyond the line of scrimmage.

pass – when the ball is thrown to a receiver who is farther down the field. A team is limited to one such forward pass per play. Normally this is the duty of the quarterback, although technically any eligible receiver can pass the ball.

play action – a type of offensive play in which the quarterback pretends to hand the ball to a running back before passing the ball. The goal is to fool the secondary into weakening their pass coverage.

play clock – visible behind the end zone at either end of the stadium. Once a play is concluded, the offense has 40 seconds to snap the ball for the next play. The duration is reduced to 25 seconds for game-related stoppages such as penalties. Time is kept on the play clock. If the offense does not snap the ball before the play clock elapses, they incur a five-yard penalty for delay of game.

punt – a kick, taken by a special teams player called the *punter*, that surrenders possession to the opposing team. This is normally done on fourth down when the offense deems gaining a first down unlikely.

receiver – an offensive player who may legally catch a pass, almost always a wide receiver, tight end, or running back. Only the two outermost players on either end of the line of scrimmage—even wide receivers who line up distantly from the offensive line—or the four players behind the line of scrimmage (such as running backs, another wide receiver, and the quarterback) are eligible receivers. If an offensive lineman, normally an ineligible receiver, is placed on the outside of the line of scrimmage because of an unusual formation, he is considered eligible but must indicate his eligibility to game officials before the play.

run – a type of offensive play in which the quarterback, after accepting the ball from center, either keeps it and heads upfield or gives the ball to another player, who then attempts to move ahead with the help of blocking teammates.

sack – a play in which the defense tackles the quarterback behind the line of scrimmage on a pass play.

safety – 1) the most uncommon scoring play in football. When an offensive player is tackled in his own end zone, the defensive team is awarded two points and receives the ball via a kick; 2) a defensive secondary position divided into two roles, free safety and strong safety.

snap – the action that begins each play. The center must snap the ball between his legs, usually to the quarterback, who accepts the ball while immediately behind the center or several yards farther back in a formation called the *shotgun*.

special teams – the personnel that take the field for the punts, kickoffs, and field goals, or a generic term for that part of the game.

tackle – 1) a term for both an offensive and defensive player. The offensive tackles line up on the outside of the line, but inside the tight end, while the defensive tackles protect the interior of their line; 2) the act of forcing a ball carrier to touch the ground with any body part other than the hand or feet. This concludes a play.

tight end – an offensive player who normally lines up on the outside of either offensive tackle. Multiple tight ends are frequently employed on running plays where the offense requires only a modest gain. Roles vary between blocking or running pass routes.

touchdown – scored when the ball breaks the vertical plane of the goal line. Worth six points, and the scoring team can add a single additional point by kick or two points by converting from the two-yard line with an offensive play.

FURTHER READING

Calamia, Ron. *FANtastic Saints*. New Orleans: FANtastic Saints, 2017.

Cohn, Nate. *New Orleans Saints*. New York: Weigl Publishers Incorporated, 2017.

Duncan, Jeff and Peter Finney. *Tales from the New Orleans Saints Sideline: A Collection of the Greatest Saints Stories Ever Told*. Victoria (BC): Sports & Recreation, 2018.

Horton, Tim. *Complete Running Back*. Champaign (IL): Human Kinetics, 2018.

Nawrocki, Nolan. *NFL Draft 2017*. Chicago: ACTA Publications, 2017.

INTERNET RESOURCES

https://www.pro-football-reference.com/players/K/KamaAl00.htm
The football-specific resource provided by Sports Reference LLC for current and historical statistics of Alvin Kamara.

https://bleacherreport.com/nfl
The official website for Bleacher Report Sport's NFL reports on each of the thirty-two teams.

https://www.cbssports.com/nfl/teams/NO/new-orleans-saints/
The web page for the New Orleans Saints provided by CBSSports.com, providing latest news and information, player profiles, scheduling, and standings.

https://www.nola.com/saints/
The web page of the *New Orleans Times-Picayune* newspaper for the New Orleans Saints football team.

http://www.espn.com/nfl/team/_/name/no/new-orleans-saints
The official website of ESPN sports network for the New Orleans Saints.

www.nfl.com/
The official website of the National Football League.

https://www.neworleanssaints.com/
The official NFL website for the New Orleans Saints football team, including history, player information, statistics, and news.

https://sports.yahoo.com/nfl/teams/neworleans/
The official website of Yahoo! Sports NFL coverage and the New Orleans Saints, providing news, statistics, and important information about the team.

A

Airheads, 58, 63
All-purpose back, 20, 22, 31–32, 37, 41, 50
Alvin Kamara Rookie of the Year Football Camp, 68
Arrest, 23
Atlanta Falcons, 62, 67

B

Baltimore Ravens, 45, 61
Bilbo, Damarius, 69
Birthday, 39, 61
Bobble heads, 54
"Boom and Zoom," 44
Brees, Drew, 11–13, 16, 55, 70
Brown, Brice, 69
Brown, Jim, 35
Buffalo Bills, 28
Bye, 34, 46

C

Camp, 68
Candy, 58, 63
Carolina Panthers, 10, 14, 27–30, 43
Charity, 67–69
Ciara, 15
Cincinnati Bengals, 25, 27–29
Cleveland Browns, 25, 62, 70
College, 22–23, 63. *See also* Hutchinson Community
    College Blue Dragons; University of Alabama;
    University of Tennessee Volunteers
Combine, 20. *See also* National Football
    League (NFL), Combine
Commercial, 55, 70
Cook, Dalvin, 27–29
Culminate, 34, 42

D

Dallas Cowboys, 69
Detroit Lions, 70
Dodson, Aaron, 51
Drake, 65
Duo, 8, 45, 52

E

Eccentric, 60, 63
Edna Karr High School, 69

F

Family, 61
Faulk, Marshall, 13, 43
Fine, 67
Fournette, Leonard, 15, 27–29, 53
French Quarter, 31, 63–64
Friends, 64–65

G

Games played, 39
Garrett, Miles, 25
George, Tollette "Tonka," 69
GoFundMe, 67
Goodell, Roger, 55
Gore, Frank, 43
Green Bay Packers, 62
Grill, 63
Grinch fundraising, 67

H

Harrison, Marvin, 40
Height/weight, 23, 39
High school, 21. *See also* Norcross
    High School Blue Devils
    football player of the year, Georgia, 21
Home, 31, 61
Hunt, Kareem, 10
Hutchinson Community College Blue
    Dragons, 7, 22–23, 42, 65–66

I

Indianapolis Colts, 25
Indispensable, 6, 8
Infraction, 60, 67
Ingram, Mark, 8, 36, 44–45, 52, 61, 67
    relationship with, 45
Injury, 7, 22–23, 65
"In My Feelings" (Drake), 65

Innovative, 48, 50
Instagram, 58

J
Jacksonville Jaguars, 10, 27, 29
"Joker" offense, 41, 50
Jones, T. J., 70

K
Kansas City Chiefs, 10
Kansas Jayhawk Community College Conference
    Offensive Player of the Year, 22
Kelly, Chad, 25
Kick returns, 19, 40

L
Landry, Jarvis, 70
Largent, Steve, 40
Lofton, James, 40
Los Angeles Raiders, 58
Los Angeles Rams, 8, 31, 46
Lutz, Will, 13
Lynch, Marshawn, 58

M
Mahomes, Patrick, 15, 53
Malone, Josh, 68
Marketing, 69–70
The Matrix, 56–57
McCaffrey, Christian, 14–15, 27–30
Media, 58
Mentor, 45, 61
Mercedes-Benz Superdome. *See* Superdome
Miami Dolphins, 11
Migos, 63–64
Mind-set, 60, 69
Minneapolis Miracle, 43
Minnesota Vikings, 8, 25, 27–29, 43
Mismatches, 34, 41
Mixon, Joe, 27–29
Morrow, Larry, 69

N
National Football League (NFL), 7–18, 35–46
    All-Pro, 39, 52
    All-Rookie, 39
    AP Offensive Rookie of the Year, 15–17, 31, 39, 53, 58
    Combine, 23
    draft, 7, 15, 23–25, 27, 31, 39, 66, 70
    Hall of Fame, 13, 18, 54
    National Football Conference (NFC), 8, 14, 43, 46, 64
    Player Care Foundation, 67
    Players Assistance Trust, 67
    playoffs, 43, 46
    Pro Bowl, 7–8, 36, 39, 45, 50, 70
    Pro Scout Combine, 23, 27
    100th anniversary, 70
    Top 100, 39
National Junior College Conference
    Association All-American, 22
New England Patriots, 25
New Orleans, 31, 42, 61–62, 64–65, 67–69
New Orleans Saints, 7, 10, 12–14, 16–18, 29, 31,
    35, 38–39, 44–46, 50–51, 53, 56, 63, 67, 70
New York Giants, 52
"Next man up," 52
Norcross, Georgia, 21, 61
Norcross High School Blue Devils, 21, 39, 42

O
Offset (Kiari), 64–65
Outback Bowl, 23
Owens, Terrell, 40–41

P
Payton, Sean, 41, 50
Payton, Walter, 18, 43
Perfetti Van Melle, 58
Performance-enhancing drugs, 45
Persona, 48, 56
Personality, 62
Philadelphia Eagles, 18, 31, 46
Piercings, 63

Platitude, 48, 52
"Play by Play" video, 58
Pokémon, 57

Q
Quavo (Quavious), 64
Quotes, 49–57

R
Receptions, 23, 35, 37, 40, 46
Redshirt, 20, 22, 45, 65
Reeves, Keanu, 57
Reeves-Maybin, Jalen, 68
Revolution Sports Group, 69
Rice, Jerry, 18
Rocky, 25

S
Saban, Nick, 22, 65
Safety, 68–69
Salary, 70
Seattle Seahawks, 15, 25, 58
Sidney Torres IV trash-collection, 70
Ski mask, 64
Smith, Emmitt, 43
Sproles, Darren, 18
Stallings Playground, 69
Stats, 23, 29, 36–37, 39–41, 43, 46
Strengths and weaknesses, 27
Sugar Bowl, 23
Super Bowl, 15, 53
          LIII, 55, 68–70
Superdome, 18, 31, 43–44, 46, 63
Surgery, 23
Suspension, 23
Sutton, Cam, 68

T
Tad Gormley Stadium, 68
Takeoff (Kirshnik), 64
Tampa Bay Buccaneers, 12, 16
Tandem, 6, 8

Tattoos, 63
Tesfatsion, Master, 56
Thomas, Michael, 70
Tomlinson, LaDainian, 18
Touchdowns, 10, 12–14, 16–17, 21–22, 35, 37, 43, 52
          first, 10–11
          receiving, 11, 23, 40, 43, 46
          rushing, 23, 29, 37, 43, 46
Trajectory, 6, 8
Turkey Giveaway and Thanksgiving Feast, 69
Twitter, 63

U
Under Armour All-America Game, 21
Uniform violation, 67
University of Alabama, 7, 22, 45, 57, 65
University of Tennessee Volunteers, 7,
          22–23, 26, 39, 42, 66, 68

V
Viral, 48–49

W
Walker, Herschel, 36
Walking to work, 31, 63–64
Walter Payton Man of the Year Award, 61
Washington Redskins, 13
Watson, Deshaun, 15, 53
Williams, Marcus, 43
Willie Hall playground recreational department, 67
Wilson, Russell, 15
Wonderlic Test, 27

Y
Yards, 11, 36, 43, 46
          all-purpose, gained by backfield duo, 8, 36, 45
          receiving, 31, 35, 40, 43, 46
          rushing, 10–11, 22–23, 29, 31, 35, 43, 46

Chapter 1

Cal Sport Media / Alamy Stock Photo
© Wellesenterprises | Dreamstime.com
Pete Sheffield | Flickr

Chapter 2

Cal Sport Media / Alamy Stock Photo
© Mbr Images | Dreamstime.com
Chad Cooper | Flickr
Chad Cooper | Flickr
JimsFlicker | Flickr
© F11photo | Dreamstime.com
Keith Allison | Flickr
Jeffrey Beall / Wikipedia Commons

Chapter 3

Cal Sport Media / Alamy Stock Photo
Jeffrey Beall / Wikipedia Commons
© Jerry Coli - Dreamstime.com
© Wisconsinart | Dreamstime.com
Jeffrey Beall / Wikipedia Commons
Keith Allison / Flickr
Cal Sport Media / Alamy Stock Photo
Cal Sport Media / Alamy Stock Photo

Chapter 4

Cal Sport Media / Alamy Stock Photo
© Vchalup | Dreamstime.com
Cal Sport Media / Alamy Stock Photo
Cal Sport Media / Alamy Stock Photo
LaDanian1000000 / Wikipedia Commons
PeakDill / Wikipedia Commons
© Zhi Qi - Dreamstime.com
© Andrii Biletskyi | Dreamstime.com

Chapter 5

Cal Sport Media / Alamy Stock Photo
© Ellesi | Dreamstime.com
Pete716 / Wikimedia Commons
© Hans Koster - Dreamstime.com
Duc Ly / Flickr
Keith Allison / Flickr
Cal Sport Media / Alamy Stock Photo

EDUCATIONAL VIDEO LINKS

CHAPTER 1

pg. 10: http://x-qr.net/1M6L

pg. 11: http://x-qr.net/1JbT

pg. 12: http://x-qr.net/1LjH

pg. 13: http://x-qr.net/1JGq

pg. 14: http://x-qr.net/1Jpv

pg. 15: http://x-qr.net/1LpF

pg. 16: http://x-qr.net/1JWn

pg. 17: http://x-qr.net/1L9F

CHAPTER 2

pg. 29: http://x-qr.net/1LBm

CHAPTER 3

pg. 44: http://x-qr.net/1JUx

CHAPTER 4

pg. 55: http://x-qr.net/1LJh

CHAPTER 5

pg. 69: http://x-qr.net/1LtA

ABOUT THE AUTHOR

Donald Parker is a father, an author, and an avid sports fan. He enjoys every type of professional sport, including NFL, NBA, MLB, and European club soccer. He enjoyed a brief career as a punter and a defensive back at the NCAA Division III level, and now spends much of his time watching and writing about the sports he loves.